Helping your Teenager
with Same-Sex
Attraction

....

Guidance for Parents and Youth
Leaders

Cooper Pinson

New
Growth
Press

newgrowthpress.com

New Growth Press, Greensboro, NC 27404
newgrowthpress.com
Copyright © 2017 by Harvest USA

Unless otherwise indicated, Scripture quotations are taken from The
Holy Bible, English Standard Version.® Copyright © 2000; 2001 by
Crossway Bibles, a division of Good News Publishers. Used by permis-
sion. All rights reserved.

Cover Design: Facout Books, faceoutstudio.com

ISBN: 978-1-945270-71-0 (Print)
ISBN: 978-1-945270-72-7 (eBook)

Library of Congress Cataloging-in-Publication Data

Names: Pinson, Cooper, author.
Title: Helping students with same-sex attraction : guidance for parents and
    youth leaders / Cooper Pinson.
Description: Greensboro, NC : New Growth Press, 2017.
Identifiers: LCCN 2017038757| ISBN 9781945270710 (single) | ISBN
    9781945270734 (5-pk)
Subjects: LCSH: Homosexuality--Religious aspects--Christianity. |
    Sex--Religious aspects--Christianity. | Church work with students. |
    Parenting--Religious aspects--Christianity. | Child rearing--Religious
    aspects--Christianity.
Classification: LCC BR115.H6 P555 2017 | DDC 261.8/35766--dc23
LC record available at https://lccn.loc.gov/2017038757

Printed in India

27 26 25 24 23 22 21 20   4 5 6 7 8

I answered my phone and heard a student's familiar voice asking if I wanted to grab dinner. He paused and then said he needed to get something off his chest. We met and shot the breeze for a couple of minutes, and then he sat in silence. After a few minutes, he reached down and pulled out a letter, "I can't get the words out, but I've written them down." He put the letter on the table and slid it slowly across to me.

I began to read his story—on page after page he shared the details of his life of guilt, shame, fear, and confusion. He was same-sex attracted and had been burdened with it for years. He had lived in isolation and had told no one.

In our world, this student's struggles are not uncommon. If you are a parent, pastor, youth group leader, and/or friend, it's likely that you know students who are wondering what to do with their romantic, erotic same-sex desires. It's also likely that those students have cowered in silence for a long time, fearing judgment and shame.

But Jesus has work to do in all of our lives, including the lives of students who struggle with same-sex attraction. As parents and youth workers, how can we partner with them in that? How do we minister to and effectively disciple students struggling with same-sex attraction? How can we, as parents, think clearly and helpfully about our own children's possible same-sex attraction? An important first step is for us to recognize that we are all more alike than we think.

Relating to the Dynamics of Same-Sex Attraction

If we, ourselves, do not experience same-sex attraction, how can we approach our students and children who are burdened in this way with compassion, empathy, and love? A good place to start is with recognizing how much we all have in common—despite our different situations and even temptations. Jesus explained this to his disciples using the metaphor of a tree and its fruit.

> "For no good tree bears bad fruit, nor again does a bad tree bear good fruit, for each tree is known by its own fruit. For figs are not gathered from thornbushes, nor are grapes picked from a bramble bush. The good person out of the good treasure of his heart produces good, and the evil person out of his evil treasure produces evil, for out of the abundance of the heart his mouth speaks." (Luke 6:43–45)

In this passage, Christ encourages us to conceptualize people organically, where life flows from the inside to the outside like a tree. This metaphor helps us see both students and ourselves in a different light.

Same-sex behavior corresponds to the fruit of the tree, but Jesus asks us to go deeper than the fruit, to discover what's going on beneath the surface. Why? Because Jesus didn't come simply to provide behavior modification. He came to transform us from the inside out. That's just as true for us as it is for the students we want to help.

The Heart (Seed)

According to Jesus, all of what we do starts with what's in our hearts: the seed of the tree. Deuteronomy 6:5 says, "You shall love the Lord your God with all your heart and with all your soul and with all your might." The heart is what the Lord is primarily concerned with in any of us, "For with the heart one believes and is justified, and with the mouth one confesses and is saved" (Romans 10:10). The heart is the mover of faith and trust. God is first and foremost concerned with where same-sex attracted students put their trust and faith. In other words, what is he or she trusting in? What does she value? What is his or her functional savior day in and day out?

This is common ground for all of us. We all feel the pull within us to pursue other gods that look more promising than Jesus. Is it the opinion of another person? The security of money? The perfect body image? To feel validated as a parent? False gods abound, and we are all drawn to them. The heart, above all, gives us the category of sinner. We are all sinners who long for other gods besides the One True God.

Context (Soil)

But the heart is not the whole story. If we tease the tree metaphor out a bit, all of us, like the tree, are planted in some kind of soil. The seed can't control the soil it's planted in; it simply receives the soil and reacts to it. Because our hearts are "planted" in a context, or an environment, that we can't control, we will naturally react to the particular context in which we find ourselves. Students, parents, youth group leaders, we all grow up in a fallen context. The list below is not meant to caricature or simplify students' stories. These soil factors also do not cause any fruit we see on the surface. However, along with our fallen hearts, the "soil" context in which we are planted *influences* the direction of our lives. Understanding these various "soil" contexts will help us better love and relate to the lives of the students we are trying to help.

Think about physical characteristics. None of us can control the body we were born with. We can influence it to a certain extent, but students can't help it if they were born stick thin or with a little extra around the middle. Still, a lot of same-sex attracted students yearn for a stereotypical body type that is epitomized by someone of the same sex. That longing, when given center-stage in a student's heart, can quickly turn into same-sex desire and lust.

Then there are family influences. No one chooses the family in which they were born, but parent and sibling relationships and the experiences and trauma that a family encounters can play a major role in how students' hearts respond.

What about personality and gifts? Many times same-sex attracted students have personalities and gifts that don't match up to the cultural norms of the society in which they live. Often they feel out of place because they don't fit into the cultural norms of being a macho guy or an ultra-feminine girl. Our masculine and

6

feminine cultural stereotypes can make students who don't fit them feel isolated and alien in a society that pushes its own norms on them. A gay life and community can look like "home" to a boy or girl who doesn't fit the gender norms of the society in which they live.

Other soil factors might include other cultural and peer influences and trauma (emotional, physical, or sexual abuse). Spiritual warfare is another soil factor: students didn't choose to be born into the war-zone of spiritual powers and authorities (Ephesians 6:12): "Your adversary the devil prowls around like a roaring lion, seeking someone to devour" (1 Peter 5:8). Our students, if they are not Christians, are "following the prince of the power of air" (Ephesians 2:2), and even Christians are constantly being pursued, influenced, and lied to by Satan.

This concept of the soil, or context, gives us another perspective alongside of the "sinner" category of the heart. Our students are not only sinners, but they are sufferers as well. And we can relate to them there. What are some things that have happened to you that have been outside of your control? How can we connect the sufferings of our own lives to the sufferings of our students?

Desires (Roots)

Roots are another important element to our tree metaphor. The roots of the tree stand for the desires that proceed from our hearts and feed on and react to the context around us.

James 1:14–15 explains it like this, "But each person is tempted when he is lured and enticed by his own desire. Then desire when it has conceived gives birth to sin, and sin when it is fully grown brings forth death."

We must remember two things here. First, even though desires can be good, while others are always evil, good desires are corrupt when they arise from a self-centered heart. In other words, the condition of our hearts determines the condition of our desires. Second, even if we are believers, good desires can be turned into false gods as we make demands of them, centering our lives around them instead of God.

Students have other intense desires beneath their attraction to those of the same sex. These desires are similar to yours: desires for companionship, validation, affection, belonging, meaning, purpose, identity, relief. Although these are non-sexual desires, they can often lead to sexual fruit and behavior.

Our desires, along with belief structures and worldviews within, help produce the multitude of sinful fruit that we see on the outside, whether it's same-sex attraction, pride, the worship of other people's opinions, or any other bad fruit. Can you relate to a student who wants companionship or a refuge from life's often-unrelenting storms? Can you relate to someone who feels that his or her identity needs to be defined by someone or something other than Jesus? Can you relate to a student who wants to follow Christ, but finds strong, competing, sinful tendencies within himself that moves him in destructive directions?

Worldviews (The Trunk)

Think about how the trunk of the tree is the necessary support for the branches and fruit of the tree. In the same way, students' worldviews hold them up; they are the pillars of their lives. Here's how Paul explains a worldview without God as the center and foundation.

> Claiming to be wise, they became fools, and exchanged the glory of the immortal God for images resembling mortal man and birds and animals and creeping things. . . . they exchanged the truth about God for a lie and worshiped and served the creature rather than the Creator, who is blessed forever! Amen. (Romans 1:22–23, 25)

Paul says at least three important things here about how our worldview affects us. First, all of us have wrong and distorted views about God. We have "exchanged the truth about God for a lie." We naturally don't worship, honor, or trust him *as* God. Second, we have wrong and distorted views about ourselves. We see ourselves as our own determiners of reality, and we think it's okay to exchange the truth about God for lies! Third, we have wrong and distorted views about other people. We worship and serve "the creature" and make "images resembling mortal man." In practice, this means that we tend to view creation, specifically other people, as little gods to be worshipped and consumed rather than loved and served.

What might the worldview narrative of a same-sex attracted student sound like?

My desires are a fundamental, identifying part of me. God is distant and can't offer me any hope for change. Another community other than the church can give me what I need.

The worldview narrative of the same-sex attracted student can sound a lot like the worldview narrative of the opposite-sex attracted student, the lonely student, or any of us! How might you view God at times that is contrary to the truth? How do you view yourself or others in fallen or distorted ways?

Manifestations of Sin (Fruit)

Our fallen hearts, planted in a fallen context with fallen desires and worldviews, eventually produce bad fruit: sinful behavior. Of course, when a student comes to Jesus, the Spirit begins to transform all of these tree aspects! First, he gives us a new heart (Ezekiel 36:26; 2 Corinthians 5:17). Even though we still struggle with sin, we can now, by the power of God, says no to our wrong desires and yes to loving God and people. In Christ, we are also given a new context. The Spirit plants us in the context of his church (1 Corinthians 12:12–31), even though he doesn't take away the fallen context in which we find ourselves. We also are given new desires that wage war against our old ones (Galatians 5:16–26). Our worldview is transformed as well (Romans 12:1–2). He supplies us with corrected and worshipful world-views about God, ourselves, and others. And he produces good fruit in us, even though we still sin!

This tree metaphor shows us that we can't pinpoint any single factor that directly determines sinful fruit, whether it's same-sex attraction or any other sin. So the tree metaphor doesn't help us so much uncover causality but rather commonality. We are all complex people, so there are multiple variables affecting each of us simultaneously. But this metaphor can give us a starting point for knowing and loving same-sex attracted students better as we approach them on common ground.

A Common Savior

Perhaps you are wondering why we need to emphasize what we all have in common. But without seeing the common ground between us, we tend to distance ourselves from each other. We are either shocked by the struggles of a same-sex attracted student, or we discount our ability to help because we don't have those same desires.

One of the wonders of the incarnation is that Jesus lived a real, human life (John 1:1–18) and experienced the temptations and sufferings that are common to us, though he was without sin (Hebrews 2:17; 4:15). Jesus knows what our lives are like. He understands us *and* is powerful to aid us.

We reflect the help, understanding, and love that Jesus gives to us by moving *toward* same-sex attracted students in empathy, compassion, and commonality, not away from them in bewilderment and fear. In some very important ways, students' stories *are* unique: they contain elements that are not shared by others. And yet, the uniqueness of a student's experience is always grounded in the commonality we all share as fellow humans in a broken and rebellious world.

When we walk alongside students with same-sex attraction or any other sexual sin, it really isn't a question about *finding* common ground. It's about *recognizing* the common ground that we already have. We both share the same fallen human condition of misplaced beliefs, desires, allegiances, and the like, and we both have access to the same divine Helper who comes close to us in love, understanding, and power. One of the first things we can do with a student is to work toward uncovering that common ground and approach Jesus together in prayer.

Now, how do we begin to build a safe ministry to same-sex attracted students? How can we, as parents, help our same-sex attracted kids? Whether we are parents or youth workers, here are some things to keep in mind.

Building a Safe Context for Same-Sex Attracted Students

Here are some things to keep in mind when building a ministry or home that facilitates the growth and discipleship of same-sex attracted students.

Talk about it. In youth ministry, whether our students hear it listed as a common struggle in our messages or conversations, or we encourage our small group leaders to discuss it, let's publicly talk about same-sex attraction and build it into our ministry vocabulary. This goes for our homes as well. As we parent, let's build a vocabulary into our homes that freely talks about both healthy, godly sexuality and the sexual brokenness that is common to humanity.

Maybe we could ask students what it would mean if a friend came out to them or confessed same-sex attraction. And then, let's encourage students to come and talk to us. From the front of our meeting rooms if we are youth ministers, or in our regular home-life if we are parents, make regular pleas to students to come to us if they wrestle with *any* sexual struggle. Maybe we can piggyback off of a pop-culture moment in a commercial, TV show, or news story that we've seen regarding same-sex issues and bring it up in conversation. But most of all, let's tell our students that we want to listen and pray with them and that we love them. And, most importantly, tell them that Jesus offers real hope to all who come to him.

Validate their suffering. It's likely that same-sex attracted students have heard many times from the church that homosexuality is simply wrong. But rarely have we acknowledged the *suffering* of the same-sex attracted student.

Suffering is an indispensable part of the Christian life, and many students might struggle with same-sex attraction for the rest of their lives. But they are not alone as suffering Christians. The Scriptures make suffering a stipulation for sharing in the coming glory of Christ: "The Spirit himself bears witness with our spirit that we are children of God, and if children, then heirs—heirs of God and fellow heirs with Christ, provided we suffer with him in order that we may also be glorified with him" (Romans 8:16–17).

Doesn't a large part of our suffering as believers have to do with the "passions of the flesh" that "wage war" against our souls (1 Peter 2:11)? All Christians are walking battlegrounds, hosts to the war between flesh and spirit. As new creations in Christ, we bear the scars. The very presence of the "flesh" waging war against our new selves and the Spirit within us means that we are sufferers.

Students who experience same-sex attraction often contend with intense loneliness, confusion, fear, and even despair as they wrestle with something that seems as if it's an essential part of who they are. We must acknowledge and enter into their pain and experience while simultaneously helping them to repent and follow Jesus.

Never say that same-sex attraction is a choice. Let's stop making it seem like students can flip a sexual light switch and change everything. None of us chose the temptations and struggles that we are stuck with for this journey. Reducing students' sexuality to a simple choice brushes aside both their stories and their complexity as individuals.

Cut out the gay jokes. Same-sex attracted students have all heard these jokes, and they are part of the reason they are in hiding. Who wants to be honest about their struggles when they are treated flippantly or the term "gay" is used in a mocking manner? As parents and youth workers, we need to eradicate any vestige of same-sex humor we might have within us and in the contexts over which we are shepherds. Same-sex attracted students need to know that they have an advocate in us.

Put an end to gender stereotypes. Not all guys love football. Not all girls love dresses. Let's show students what real men and women look like, constantly teaching against unhelpful masculine and feminine stereotypes. Instead let's teach our students what true men and women look like in the kingdom of God. Real men and women leave everything, denying even themselves, to follow after Jesus (Luke 9:23–25). Real men don't always have six-pack abs and hunt animals. Not all real woman like getting a mani-pedi and going out for lunch.

Our ministry to students must be varied and rich, recognizing, validating, and fostering the unique, God-given gifts our students possess.

Keep the main thing the main thing. Students need to hear that the opposite of homosexuality and the goal of the Christian life is not heterosexuality but the holiness that flows from trusting and loving Christ (Hebrews 12:14). Yes, God's design and intention for humanity is heterosexuality, but heterosexuality doesn't solve the problem of sin. And because of our sin, even our heterosexuality is distorted and used to rebel against God. We are after one main thing in ministering to our students: Christ-likeness (Romans 8:29).

Helping a Same-Sex Attracted Student

As we begin to cultivate a godly ministry and home for same-sex attracted students, a natural question follows: how should we think about engaging particular same-sex attracted students who want to follow Jesus? How can we encourage them to grow as followers of Christ? A ministry and home that can effectively disciple students who struggle with same-sex attraction must have broad principles in mind, but it must also have more specific principles to implement with any particular student who comes for help. What are some specific ways to help?

Set up a regular time to meet. Since we know that sexual fruit is only the surface of the issue, we need to set aside time for those same-sex attracted students who are hurting to get to know, love, and understand them. For a same-sex attracted student, you are probably one of the first, and the few, in whom he or she has confided. This student needs to see that you are willing to take the time to know and walk with him or her and that you won't spook at the first sign of danger, messiness, shame, or guilt.

Empathize. We are called to come near to understand, suffer alongside of (Romans 12:15), and forgive as those who have been forgiven (Colossians 3:13). This means recognizing that same-sex attracted strugglers are not a problem to be solved but fellow sojourners on life's journey. As we do this we are reflecting Christ to him or her. Hebrews 4:15 tells us something beautiful about the person of Christ, "For we do not have a high priest who is unable to sympathize with our weaknesses, but one who in every respect has been tempted as we are, yet without sin." Notice that what uniquely qualifies Jesus to help us from this passage is not his divinity; it's his humanity. As a human, he has been tempted as we are. He knows our weaknesses. He has felt them and been burdened by them. In the same way, when we empathize with our students, feeling with them the intensity and commonness of their struggle, we reflect a strong and compassionate picture of Christ to them.

Listen and learn. Use the tree metaphor to discover students' stories. Spend some time asking questions about each part of their life experience. Map the tree onto their lives. For Christians, same-sex attraction tends to be simply an abstract, cultural issue. But same-sex attraction is always embodied in a particular person's story. Each student has a unique story; a unique makeup. We *must* ask good questions about their lives, experiences, sorrows, and joys if we want to help them see Christ and connect him to the details of their story. Remember, the tree metaphor helps us discover our commonality, but it does not obliterate uniqueness. One of the balancing acts of ministering to and loving people well is taking seriously both what you have in common and what makes them unique.

James reminds us to "let every person be quick to hear, slow to speak, slow to anger" (James 1:19). Let's be quick to listen to our students and their stories. Ultimately, we are to imitate the intimate and personal care with which Jesus shepherds us.

Here are some questions you may want to explore with students:

- How has their struggle with same-sex attraction affected their lives in the past and present?
- How has their context affected them throughout their lives, both for good and for bad?
- What are some worldviews they have had in the past and have now regarding God, themselves, and others?
- When a student says, "I'm gay," what does he or she mean by that? How does that affect the way they see their identity?

Give them a realistic view of the Christian life. Don't be afraid to let students and your own children know what the Christian life is really like. As we've seen above, a life spent following Jesus is going to be difficult: cross-carrying difficult. Pretending that the Christian life will be full of unfettered, earthly happiness and carefree living is not a biblical message. For a same-sex attracted student, that suffering has a particular bent. Christ could change this student's desires completely, replace same-sex desire with heterosexual desire, or could even give a student exclusive desires for only one person of the opposite sex. Or Christ could never give heterosexual desires. Christ could also call the same-sex attracted student to a life of singleness and celibacy. The point to remember is that the goal of the Christian life is holiness, not marriageable heterosexuality.[1]

Christ offers us real hope on this side and the other side of eternity. He promises to be at work through every circumstance and to be present through every suffering. And here's the important part: Jesus will, by his Spirit, make us more like him and will increasingly give us a greater love for him as we grow in holiness (1 Thessalonians 5:23–24). He guarantees it (Philippians 1:6)! And as he is at work in us, he promises that he will be with us (Matthew 28:20) and will come back for us (John 14:1–3).

Give them a vocabulary for the Christian life. Along with this realistic view of the Christian life, we must build for same-sex attracted students a real, Christian vocabulary. The Christian life is lived by daily *faith*, *repentance*, and *love* (Mark 1:14–15; Matthew 22:37–40): we must daily reorient our trust around the person of Christ, daily turn from our sins to follow him, and daily love others by practically serving them. Daily *self-denial* lived in faith, repentance, and love is the means the Spirit uses to grow us in love for God and others.

We also have to help same-sex attracted students understand that change and growth in godliness is a *process*, a daily fight to turn from our sin and turn again to Jesus through prayer; reading, meditating on, and even memorizing Scripture; being in open and honest relationships with other Christians; and serving others.

Another part of the vocabulary of Christian living is *identity*. If our students are in Christ, we need to help them see that same-sex attraction doesn't define them. Students, like all of us, wonder: *Who am I? Am I defined by my intense, fallen desires? Am I defined by the temptations that keep assaulting me?*

It's helpful to read what Paul says in 1 Corinthians 6:9–11. He begins, "Do not be deceived: neither the sexually immoral, nor idolaters, nor adulterers, nor men who practice homosexuality, nor thieves, nor the greedy, nor drunkards, nor revilers, nor swindlers will inherit the kingdom of God." Paul is not saying here that those sins disqualify us from being Christians. Instead he is saying that those who accept and embrace their sins and struggles as their identity have no stake in the glorious future of the Kingdom.

Then Paul goes on: "And such *were* some of you. But you were washed, you were sanctified, you were justified in the name of the Lord Jesus Christ and by the Spirit of our God" (v. 11, emphasis added). For those who have trusted in Jesus, their identity *is* washed, sanctified, and justified, all in the name of Christ and because of his Spirit's work. Paul is writing to all who claim the name of Jesus. He is reminding us that our sins and fallen tendencies no longer define us; Jesus does.

Youth culture, like most of life, is in a search for identity. If students buy into and adopt identities not given to them by their heavenly Father, they cheapen the true identity they have in Christ and deprive themselves of a strong motivation to continue the fight against sin. If students are trusting in Jesus, they are more secure than their temptations would lead them to believe. They are his, and no struggle can change

20

that. We need to constantly remind ourselves and the students in our care that we are not defined by our sins and temptations. We are washed, sanctified, and justified. We are children of the living God in the name of Jesus Christ. That's who we are. Now. Forever.

Help them grow in community. Same-sex attraction is one of the most taboo issues in the church today. Students who experience SSA, perhaps more so than any other sexual issue, struggle in the church to grow in openness and community. And they have good reasons for it: most of us in the church have treated them as outcasts and untouchables. The imperative is clear: We *must* help students grow in the life-giving community of the church.

Part of our job in ministering to and loving same-sex attracted students is to help them open up about their temptations and sins to other godly, safe people. This isn't going to happen right away, nor should it. But along with encouraging them to live out of the grace of God and in their identity as child of God, you should also help them to identify other safe people who they can share their struggles with.

This doesn't mean that they should be fully transparent with everyone. There are many people out there to whom it would not be safe to disclose same-sex attraction. Still, we want to help students identify trusted people in their own lives who they can walk with in openness and community. If you are a youth worker, you also want to encourage students to confide in their parents. This can be a wonderful way to help shepherd families instead of simply individuals. If you are a parent, it might be good to encourage your older child to talk to a trusted youth worker or volunteer.

Having this broadening circle of transparency counteracts the fear, shame, and isolation that come with sexual struggles and can, as we confess our sins to one another, work to heal us (James 5:16).

Help them grow in love and ministry. Same-sex attracted students are not second-class citizens in the kingdom of God. Like the rest of us, they have been given gifts to contribute to the building up of the body of Christ. Let's help them discover, develop, and implement those gifts in love and ministry to others.

Same-sex attracted students' gifts oftentimes do not match the gender-stereotyped views of the culture in which they live. This is more than okay! The real question is: what gifts has God given them, and how can they, in turn, use them for his glory? While doing this, we are validating the real place same-sex attracted students have in the kingdom of God.

Here's the vision: What would it look like for a football-loving father to invest in his same-sex attracted son's passion for art, taking him out to museums, encouraging him to take art classes, and being excited and interested in the God-given talents his son is passionate about?

Point them to Jesus. As we love same-sex attracted students, we need to constantly point them to their Savior. First, we need to be reminding students that they *live* in Jesus. Ephesians 2:5 says that God "made us alive" in Christ. Same-sex attracted students who trust in Jesus are not dead in their sins. They have been radically made alive in Christ. There has been a definitive break with their old way of life, and now they truly live in Christ (Romans 6:1–11). They are "new creations," regardless of whether they feel like it or not (2 Corinthians 5:17).

Second, for same-sex attracted students who trust in Jesus, they have *received* the Spirit of Christ, meaning Christ has poured out the Spirit on them (Acts 2:33) and he, by his Spirit, lives within them (Romans 8:9–11). The Spirit will work and change them over time as they pursue Jesus. God will not give up on them. When no change seems to be happening, Jesus is always working by his Spirit.

Third, for same-sex attracted students who trust in Jesus, they *will be* with Jesus. Salvation is not reversible. They cannot lose what has been granted to them in Christ. When the kingdom of God comes in power, all sin will be no more, and our sexuality will be fully redeemed forever:

> And I heard a loud voice from the throne saying, "Behold, the dwelling place of God is with man. He will dwell with them, and they will be his people, and God himself will be with them as their God. He will wipe away every tear from their eyes, and death shall be no more, neither shall there be mourning, nor crying, nor pain anymore, for the former things have passed away." (Revelation 21:3–4)

Their current identity in Jesus, the empowering work of the Spirit, and the future glory toward which they are headed will be strong motivations to keep running hard after Christ. As students begin to live by daily faith, repentance, and love, they will begin to be transformed by Christ's Spirit into beautiful reflectors of his image, slowly producing good fruit as they walk with Jesus and look toward being with him forever.

As we seek to build ministries, homes, and relationships that are Christ-honoring for same-sex attracted students, we have the wonderful opportunity to help students see that Jesus speaks into and infiltrates all areas of life and brokenness. No struggle is outside of his redemption. As we pursue Jesus, he guarantees that one day we will meet him face to face. On that day, all sin, suffering, and darkness will be dispelled, and we will be with our Savior, to live, love, and worship him for all eternity.

Endnotes

[1] For a fuller discussion of this point, see David White's minibook, *Can You Change If You Are Gay?* (Greensboro, NC: New Growth Press, 2013).